ALSO BY STEPHANOS PAPADOPOULOS

POETRY

Hôtel-Dieu

Lost Days

TRANSLATIONS

Poems, Selected Poems of Derek Walcott
(Into Greek with Katerina Anghelaki-Rooke)

THE BLACK SEA

THE BLACK SE

Poems

Stephanos Papadopoul

For Derek Walcott

Designed and typeset by The Sheep Meadow Press

Cover designed by Paul Stechschulte
Author photo courtesy of Franco Capponi, Civitella Ranieri

Distributed by The University Press of New England

All inquiries and permission requests should be addressed to the publisher:

The Sheep Meadow Press
PO Box 84
Rhinebeck, NY 12572

Library of Congress Cataloging-in-Publication Data

Papadopolous, Stephanos, 1976-
  The Black Sea / Stephanos Papadopoulos.
    p. cm.
  ISBN 978-1-937679-09-5
I. TITLE.
  PS3566.A598B53 2012
  811'.54--DC23

                              2012037196

TABLE OF CONTENTS

AUTHOR'S NOTE

After WWI and the signing of the Treaty of Lausanne in 1923, a policy of "population exchange" was adopted between Greece and Turkey in which both Turks and Greeks were "repatriated" to their original homelands respectively. This absurd concept essentially legalized the ethnic cleansing that had been taking place since 1915. When this coincided with disastrous notions of Greek military expansion, the result was horror on an unimaginable scale. Atrocities occurred on both sides since the Turks from Northern Greece were also deported, but the ethnic cleansing of Greeks from Anatolia and the Black Sea region was particularly brutal and systematic. By 1915 the Armenians had already been purged from the new Turkish state, and between 1916 and 1923 the Southern Black Sea coast was virtually emptied of its Greeks. There were death marches into the mountains, massacres, rapes, and a human displacement that led to one of the largest humanitarian and refugee crises in Southern Europe.

My great-grandfather was a Greek tobacco merchant from the city of Samsun on the Black Sea coast. My grandfather was born there in 1888, but moved westward to Sinope, Constantinople, Greece, then briefly Paris, where he studied couture, and eventually returned and settled in Athens, where he repatriated his remaining family. Other relatives ended up in Russia and Northern Greece. I have taken fragments of true stories and anecdotes from my own family's history in the region, and mixed them freely with imagined lives from scrapbooks, postcards, photographs as well as historical documentation and firsthand accounts.

I recently traveled from Greece, through Anatolia and back along the length of the Southern Black Sea coast, exploring the landscapes, cities and villages in which many of these events took place. I am no scholar or historian and this is by no means a history of the Black Sea. I am not interested in making nationalistic or political statements about an event that is already charged with emotion on all sides. These are simply poems about people and suffering, an homage to a generation of exiles, all victims of the futility of war.

S. P
New York, New York
2012

"As from the 1st May, 1923, there shall take place a compulsory exchange of Turkish nationals of the Greek Orthodox religion established in Turkish territory, and of Greek nationals of the Muslim religion established in Greek territory. These persons shall not return to live in Turkey or Greece respectively without the authorization of the Turkish Government or of the Greek Government respectively."

Excerpt from the Treaty of Lausanne, 1923

THE BLACK SEA

THE POET

He walks naked to the window,
looks out across the city, the ancient walls,
the trawlers cinched tight along the promenade,
the dogs sleeping in clusters among the piled nets
and the first hint of light that arrives,
messenger between the hours of sleep, thin line
that holds the horizon to its edge, that holds
his throat to the horizon so that every vista
is a lanyard over-tightened, a clothesline tied
to the olive tree and swallowed by its bark,
a dream he left that followed him in daylight,
oil lamps burning for the blind, fireflies at dawn,
pain's logic, the lantern in the midday sun—
he dresses slowly like the hangman.

MELANTHE SPEAKS TO GOD

All night the sea flutters like tin,
ex-voto for the sulfurous zone, dead
as the mute black sky and the stars too thin.
A wish on something falling sinks like lead;
that's what I think, made my wishes
and wore the paint of icons on my lips.
The priest intones that he who washes
in the holy water is rid of lies.
That's the language of men, full of solutions.
I buried three children in the cold dawn
by the roadside without prayer or ablutions
and heaped the stones to hold their bodies down
and kept walking through that field of stolen corn
whose husks are paper crosses on the cairn.

VOICES

Black Sea South Coast

Voices still rise from foggy hillsides
that drop and fade into the shore of this Black Sea,
sulfurous and dead beneath the upper zone of life
where fish once roiled in silver clouds
and one too many mythic rivers met
in water ringed by mountains without names,
before Ionia, Anatolia,
before Ovid pined for Rome and wept in Tomi,
and Xerxes whipped the straits with chains,
before Thales, Heraclitus, Anaximander,
that army of gadflies and madmen
looked into the sun with arrogance,
before men fought for this view from an open window,
and the harbors burned for the love of burning.

An Oval Photograph

Uncle Constantine, great uncle sadly unmet,
your cream suits are forever pressed to perfection,
with hands like the folded wings of sleeping birds,
soft eyes fixed on some unknown distance,
the phantom limbs of childhood streets.
Constantine, you knew the wind's caprice,
the names of rivers, the fashions in France,
walked with a cane and banded sun hat
on the unused sands of Athenian beaches.
The fire red sunsets over the Bosphorus
carried in your veins, your sadness
wrapped in cream linen and delicate sheets
of writing paper light as air, letters unsent,
bottles of ink unopened, the sleep of unturned pages.

Rain Over Trabzon

Heavy raindrops strike the water,
a wafer of dissolving sunlight below the clouds
is a white line on a canvas of storm-blue.
The rain erases and renews itself in puddles
that lean like oval mirrors on the promenade
where the priest hurries, robes lifted from his ankles,
thin white ankles reflected in the rain pools,
dark sky over Trabzon, the mist filtering
through streets exchanged like dirty banknotes,
Rubles, Drachmas, Lira, passed hand to hand,
the dog-eared corners wet with blood, bent
by angry fingers, angry men with sadder wives,
the streets of Trebizond, Trabzon, Trapezounda
washed by rain but won't wash clean.

ARISTOTELES' JEREMIAD

"There was trouble on both sides" —his eyebrow raised
like a tent frame falls again in place.
"Some want to hear their nation's glory praised
as though the sound of trumpets has no price.
Friend, the people are dumb blind beasts
fired up over thoughts that were planted
like some cash crop in their brains,
and before long, they'd have rather parted
with their children than leave the battle trench."
His cigarette curls Virginia smoke.
"Heads rolled while Smyrna burned and the foreigners
 stood idly on navy ships and joked,
then asked for lunch. All nations are shits."
He turns from a stuffed ashtray and spits.

The Circassian Whore

These blond locks are worth a pretty penny, boy.
The Turkman thinks my ass is his, the Greeks are beasts.
But a glass of this sweet wine will bring them to their knees.
Greeks, Turks, whatever—two half-wits make a man, I guess.
I've spread these thighs for seven armies
and when they come to fuck the flags are gone.
I've seen a thousand pricks that look the same to me.
But what do I know, a whore in a broken world?
A little hash for better dreams is all I want
and a jar of rosewater for my hair.
Let them un-conjure their fat wives when they heave inside me.
I'm paid and they'll soon be dead, we'll all be gone
and these fields will grow wild with poppies
always faithful to the color red.

THE DEAD SPEAK TO THE PASSING TRAVELER
Hills of Samsun

We've behaved, gone on stuffed in graves,
mouths filled with rain or the summer's furnace
that swells our skulls, and priestly games—
visions that no longer fool us.
In God our faith was placed before it failed,
the letters browned then turned to powder,
never sent—our coffins soon were nailed.
The story needs a mouth to hold its power.
Follow the road by the mule cart tracks
to where the earth bleeds a thick red rust
from iron seeping down the mountain trails,
and for a second stop and think of us,
tell it from this spot where we were chained,
our deaths like marriages arranged.

ALEKOS

The dawn is a moon sliver in his eyes,
an ice chip that melts into the Western haze,
brief as the ultraviolet star that consumes it.
The boats groan against their chains,
the cats scream on roof tiles
in shuttered streets where the stones
are tossed like broken teeth.
He doesn't want philosophy
but these slow daybreaks make him thoughtful
and the cigarettes taste better in the dark
when he sits and hears the sea moving in,
and the blackness masks the skeletal houses
charred in the port and the bodies of the dead
heaped on street corners, nosed by hungry dogs.

THE PASHA'S LAMENT

Kerasounda, 1920

Black dogs and infidels who won't sit down—
I've given them everything yet the bastards
keep rising and clawing at my throat, damn
these surly people, I've done my best,
damn this wretched, godforsaken post
with the salt sea wind chewing at my bones.
Life keeps slipping, the days run past
like shadow plays, and my heart burns
for sweetness, not some Circassian whore
whose serpent tongue has swindled legions.
A barrelful of hacked Greek ears I swore
I'd send the Sultan as allegiance,
sliced off in battle and pickled in brine…
Lord, my head spins…bring me more wine!

THE BLACK SEA HISTORY

Black night, but the moon rises and the whitebait leap
in spasmic clouds of mercury from the sea.
Like a dropped shield, the water faces the sky
with the cedar bones of the pier rotting, salt-bound,
leaning into the water, shadows carved
with thick black lines against the smoldering skyline.
For centuries dark eyes have fished this poisoned deep,
blind to the dark below the hundred meter mark
where the dead begin and the rivers dump their silt
that stuffs the strangled Bosphorus.
One day all the scattered boats that line the harbor
will sink with hulls rammed full of holes
through which the moon will shine its cargo
on the cold sea bed where nothing moves.

THE MARCH FROM HARPOOT TO MALATIA
September 1, 1917

We walk, cold eyes, chained animals walking
with our gaze bolted to the plane of the sea.
Stubborn, the sun rises, then strikes the water.
The sky is a bandage stained with memory.
Once this was called beautiful,
poets sang for the streaming fire show,
violins tore their strings on the rain-stamped ashes
and the broken temples of Anatolia,
our love, uncorrupted, was plain as bread—
but the stubble fields of planted shallow graves
will not yield, our striking daughters have grown beards,
they walk with hollow bones like the sea birds,
they leave the poppy in the roadside dust
which covers every living thing for miles.

Amisos

Samsun, 1922

Everything is beautiful and fatal in this port—
the doors of the Greek houses swing in the wind,
the scrape of soldiers boots scar the quiet streets.
At dusk the sea goes mauve and the jetty melts
into the water as the vowels rip
from minarets and the muezzin's cry
swims from one rooftop to the next,
the evening prayer trapped by mountains,
splashing back through alleys toward the sea.
Such sad confusion in that sound, when half
the city kneels and prays while the other cringes,
and in the flat harbor the whitebait rise to the surface
by the thousands, dripping silver from the nets
to feed the army, hungry from its work.

SAVAS ON THE WHITE HORSE

How unbound we are by that same smoke,
the taste of the dead on our tongues,
with the sun that leaks into the valleys
and feeds the fields below now gone to weeds.
His mustache was a crossbar bolted shut.
At the sound of the hooves, his brothers stood
and waited at attention for his entrance;
they were statues in the dark,
each act a shadow seen though lock and key,
a tragedy without transcendence.
From Samsun on his old white horse,
Savas rode in across the fields;
his pockets were filled with tobacco,
Christ, the color of those golden leaves!

The Poet in the Harbor

He likes to go down to the harbor late
when the shutters of the town are latched
and nothing breathes but the sea swell,
the machinery of stars that remind and repeat
those things he knows but can't explain,
a place beyond the pain of human voices.
He likes to lie down in the mounds of fishnets
with the dogs, with the ghosts of dolphins
snared by negligence, by careless ropes cut loose,
by a second in which joy becomes abandon
and abandon, as it never fails to do,
enters the realm of tragedy, and so he likes
to go down there alone and fall asleep
in the nets with the dogs and the reek of the sea.

ARISTOTÉLIS SINGS HIS TESTAMENT

Trabzon, 1919

Fuck the pencil-necked merchants and their fat wives
swaddled in thrice-coveted linens and fancy threads
whose scraping and bowing makes my stomach churn.
I'd sooner see their heads staked at the gates of Smyrna
than their buttered thighs crossed on the Sultan's pillows.
They call me Telis and the skin on my chest
waits for the bullet that will bleed me in the field.
I'll go gladly, draped like rags on the barbed wire,
with lead in my bones and blood blacker than these streets
whose beauty is the unwrapped pain of generations.
You can keep your saddled horses and your promises,
your guaranteed safe passage and your paid-for goodbyes.
I'll hold my course to where the sun rises over Pontic hills
with powder smoke and knives. Go dry your damned eyes.

MELANTHE SPEAKS OF MARRIAGE

Syros, 1926

I was fifteen when childhood went away
and never returned, though I called it back.
My marriage was arranged, I had no say.
An unknown man arrived; I was told to pack.
That's how things happen, the rest is a waste
and better left to mandolins and lyres.
For years I never saw my husband's face
and the few who spoke for peace were liars
and proven wrong they left their broken wives,
plowing them like angry bulls for child,
then fleeing to the hills again with wolves
to fight the war and losing turning wild;
those lucky ones who got to die and sleep
in graves I left, in photographs I keep.

THE BROTHERS LONG MARCH

Black Sea – Russia, 1920

Two brothers hauled a chest full of rubles,
across the dead towns of Anatolia
to eastern beaches with Ovid's ghost,
and into Russia with the advancing snow.
Under cold sunsets they watched the road freeze,
and the bare nets of branches in treetops
rattle with their heavy shags of ice,
speaking little, as if their tongues had dried.
They dragged their paper treasure through snowfields,
a wooden coffin packed with minted landscapes,
mute generals, frail lithographs of statesmen
whose profiles were the archipelagos of war.
Barefoot, they reached the Caucasus where piles
of worthless banknotes burned in the streets.

OLD ARISTOTELIS SPEAKS FROM THE CAFÉ

Trabzon, 1918

"The pain returns where the horizon ends,"
says the eye spinning fish-like in its socket.
"To hell with your present and your future tense—
we live hand to mouth, they, from hand to pocket.
I'm old and this generation's for the birds.
Burning sticks and ashes is all that will be left.
Our grandfathers carried knives and grew their beards,
drank wine unwatered like real mountain *klefts*.
'O lay my sad bones with sweet Melpo…'
whine the boys with goose down on their faces.
Goddamn these cosmopolitan ideas!
To the guns my boys if you're not disgraces,
It's blood in the dirt and more of the same."
Aristotelis growls, and bangs his cane.

THE BURNED FIELDS AT SAMSUN

The sun bleeds into another morning
quiet as the dead and the dead to be
who slip from shadow to shifting shadow
with their scars still pink as the dawn that drives
them underground, sometimes for centuries.
The earth dries—the trees that sheltered eyes
and umbrella'd the rain in September
were chopped and burned to smoke
that climbs into the airless sky and blooms
dark shapes across this thing called history,
which to us is just the pain of losing.
But the mornings still come and nothing's lit
in this landscape that refuses to speak
with its gods rubbing ashes from their eyes.

MELANTHE SPEAKS OF HER LONG MARCH
Toward Sebasteia, 1919

I felt the child in my belly like lead.
It was sinking, I asked the lord to take it fast,
stamp out the sun because I'm better dead
than left this damaged shell. I'll be last,
anything to close my eyes and rest
and never look again. "At what?" you say.
This horizon cuts like a knife. It's best,
to look no longer now, that's the way,
you take your pick, the gun, the fist, the axe.
I felt the blade, another, cold as eyes
that stared me from my home and turned their backs
when weeping I went out—they saw my size,
saw me fall and saw the road turn red, but blind
they knifed it, told me not to fall behind.

ALEKOS REMEMBERS SMYRNA

Athens, 1929

They carried us down to those trawlers
and there were no bright waves,
no breath of wind to fill our ragged sails,
just the oily port and the women's veils.
The deeper the sadness, the longer the silence.
The blank faces lined the boat rails,
the dead sank and made no sound.
On land the dirt remains, the smoke trails
from the footprints of torched houses, a burnt taste—
this is the blackened bread of memory.
Try and remember? It's nothing but waste—
You want to count the dead? One is too many.
You want the lesson history gave?
Each field furrow is an open grave.

STAVROS, COUTURIER

Athens

If a stitch were missing or a pocket skewed,
he would tear a suit in half, without a word;
this is how you learn, is what his eyes said,
while they measured and pinned and chalked at work.
There was integrity in a clean cut
of English wool, a kind of sanity
in every metered nuance of the craft.
A man's corrected hunch was never vanity,
but simply an advance of patience,
as though a suit were never really sold
but lent to certain shoulders for practice
because the master himself, though bold
isn't sure the lines are right when shoulders shift,
when nothing else but doubt preserves the gift.

THE GHOSTS OF THE OPEN FIELDS

The open fields are constantly at war,
the raw hands, the rusted pail
turn the earth as if it weren't
chalk dust where crops will fail.
These backs in the borrowed field
have always lived on hands and knees,
coaxing a little barley, pathetic yield,
halved again by the Pasha's fees.
The wheat replaced with tobacco rows,
when smoke earns more than what there is to eat,
there's nothing left here that grows,
just these shadows with their swollen feet,
breaking the stones resignedly;
where the wheat dwindles like an army.

POSTCARDS FROM RUSSIA

Moscow

Tinted postcards were the signature of exile,
faces in the Russian snow with minarets
rising like air balloons in pale horizons,
and the expressions held for the slow camera
are the face-lines of prisoners, and the pastels
rouge their cheeks and brightly color the air
with swirls of green, garlands of exotic flowers
and parrots that sail the glazed Moscow skyline.
"Love, and above all, health to the family at home,"
writes the careful hand in borrowed ink.
The tongue licks the stamp, the card is sent.
Their breath is the beat of the turning page,
the dust that slips from book spines,
their mouths are angry drawers sliding shut.

The Pasha Can't Sleep

Kerasounda, 1920

Drowning in furs, his tassled fez a gash
of red as though his head is dripping blood;
he stares at the sea through apple-scented smoke
and won't speak. The eunuch brings more drink.
He won't touch food, the women go home cold.
His eyes are windows reflecting the passing birds.
At night, shutters drawn and the fire high
he lurches with the shadows on the wall.
He doesn't sleep, his mind is crammed with ghosts
dragging their children through the gates
of towns wrecked into memory.
The wine soothes and cools his aching throat,
it hisses through the fever and rises
in the blood rims and veins of his eyes.

THE CIRCASSIAN WHORE RECOUNTS
HER DREAM

I was in the city…which? There is no other.
There were lights on the water and the little boats
twinkled with their lanterns setting out in the dark.
There was wine and my cheeks were candy red
under the acacia trees, we were walking hand in hand.
He was no common sailor, there were stripes on his shoulders
and his mustache gleamed with beeswax in the lamplight.
From his head curled a black breaking wave of hair.
The bank notes rolled from his pocket like music,
and once that golden clip was pulled, they fell on me,
sweet rain, with his fingers growing bold and the scent
of apple smoke and jasmine from the open window…
O, those hands uncalloused by the dirty plow!
Those blue eyes undarkened by the killings!

WALKING TO SEBASTEIA

The light arrives in sullen masquerade
yet the body moves on built-in code,
and the heart's dumb repetition
drives them into deeper snow.
They march and will keep marching
till the last child dies and the mothers stop.
Down the line, across unopened boxes,
through the floods and fire that unfolds
like a single flower in Sebasteia
yet burns with a glutton's fervor
where the women walk like dead machines,
a boar, psychopathic, blind,
feeds face down in this trough,
where the sun won't go.

CAPTAIN MARKOS

One-legged I fished this sea
and each red lipped wave
that snarled at me
I snarled it back.
I've seen these nets thick
with cold blue bodies
and I'm not talking fish—
the sea is salt and blood.
From Sinope's rocks I've sailed
with these two arms for legs,
the oars my walking sticks.
Only the murdered will float.
What was meant to swim
and ain't a boat, has fins.

ROADS

Who knows what he saw in the height of summer,
alone with the dust in his eyes and the wind that howled
through the graveled roads of these coastal towns.
He walked bare-headed and empty-handed,
toward those smiles, thin descending slashes
glimpsed through a parted door and door frame.
He knew the animals didn't care for conversation,
they huddled and dropped their pellets on the mountainside,
a maddened herd in the road with their ears laid back,
snorting and stomping in scattered brush. The sea,
a bowl of dishwater grey. In its face
the flash of migrating birds, the hands
which cupped it, washed the dust from their legs,
washed the blood into the metallic earth.

THE PASHA SUMMONS THE CIRCASSIAN

We're more alike than it may seem, he grins.
She stands in the dark lit by her eyes,
the same green shade of her scarf that is no accident,
nor the wheat-colored curl that strays from it.
She nods but never smiles. I turn my back,
he says, for the Sultan and the Greeks;
those pests keep gnawing at me, but they live—
right now I'd rather fuck than fight.
He pulls her close, his finger draws a line
across her thigh, the scarf comes loose.
I love war as much as you love men, he says
and winks, dropping a wet chunk of hash
on the smoldering coals of the pipe.
She opens her gown, blows out the light.

The Lost Armies

Once again snow covered the barley fields
where not a seed remained unscavenged on the stalk.
Mithridates, Xenophon and Alexander marched;
Xerxes and Tamurlane dragged their armies down
like starving dogs across these stones and open tombs
and when the bread was gone they killed their horses,
broke their teeth on hooves, sucked the bones,
boiled their saddles and drank the broth.
Their bronchitic chests burned, desert madness,
broken, they lived for gold, wine, women, uncut wine.
Wild young men named these cities, hammered stakes,
boundaries soon effaced by sand, their drinking;
their love songs and dirges, unwritten and now unsung,
are wind on these plains of Anatolia.

THALASSA

The road leads toward the splintered sun.
A shrub leaps into a single conifer.
Suddenly there are two conifers, then three.
They multiply into a forest.
The forest dwindles, falls in squares
of furrowed earth and farms begin.
Tobacco grows, the supple hills are brown.
They bend into the blueish mountains.
Beyond the mountains lies the water
where the army of ten-thousand stopped,
untied their helmets, dropped their shields,
crashed to their knees and held their heads
at the line of curved blue water,
so wide, so deep, so dead.

BROTHERS

They took their names from generals and kings.
Epaminondas, Constantine,
those titles, steel cages hauled,
the transient grasping for permanence,
the uprooted renaming their roots.
Water and oil, they trembled on the surface,
two brothers raced across an open field
and then one kneeled and watched
a sudden rose bloom on his chest
where the lead thumped through his rib cage
and cracked against his spine.
He warned the other with his eyes
who understood and held the gaze
then turned and ran toward the sea.

ALEKOS AND THE PILGRIMAGE TO SUMELÁ

It took us thirty days along the coast
through the mountains from Sinope
to Amisos with her crumbling walls,
and harbor all ablaze with colored boats
and sunlight bright as Mary's robe
at the monastery Sumelá near Trabzon.
The Turks, they called her *Mariamáma*,
and washed their feet and kneeled before her too;
our voices lived strangely together in the hills,
the smoke boiled softly from our stoves.
We wore our crosses in the mountain roads
and drank our tea with big-faced farmers;
our blood was sugar mixed with leaves
that flutter and eventually settle in the glass.

THE MONK VISITS THE ABANDONED
MONASTERY   *Sumela Monastery, Trebizond*

He struggles down the path from Sumela
where the monastery claws the rock and hangs
with its company of saints, eyes gouged out
as the centuries of blindness begin.
He knows the sound of rushing water
as it hurtles toward the valley, he knows
the shadow of the falcon, the crow's cry,
the bat's erratic swoop as evening comes.
He knows the sound of the bells clanging
through the abandoned peaks,
the spoon's scrape against the bottom
of a copper bowl, and the breeze,
which used to carry the hint of beeswax and pine,
stinks like a dead crow in the canyons.

THE WIDOW'S SONG

Every village hides a widow in the know.
Black stockings on the clothesline show
the scurvied knees that used to dance.
She says, I married, I'm no dunce.
Did I choose muscles and a thick mustache?
Hell no! Don't be surprised, but I'm no ass.
I looked for a survivor, you can see it in the eyes.
Men do a lot of talking; don't ever trust your ears.
Mine said he was a captain, I figured good escape!
When those fools started on about a nation state
I knew that it was time to pack the bag.
I may look old and dumb, but this hag
knew more about the war than all the raving males.
Your David and Goliaths are built for fairy tales.

THE ADMIRAL VISITS THE CIRCASSIAN

St. Francis would weep for that green-eyed bitch,
her yellow halo scattered on the bed—
I thought I'd drown myself between her thighs.
She never said a word, just dropped her eyes
and stood there naked as the lamp flame
like Praxiteles' Venus, broken free.
Christ, she lay back cool, pale, disinterested;
which broke my lust into rage instead.
No army frightens like the thoughts in her head,
and so I punished her for her absence
but she turned and laughed when I lay empty,
unable to go on, still taunting me
with open legs, her hair unkempt—
I pulled a pillow to my face, and wept.

THE REFUGEES

The crowds walk down the paths
to broken piers, their eyes are tar
where the moon's dull reflection rides,
last lamp of the Pontic kings, last light
for the refugees before they board,
before the oars tear the upset water
and the water swells against the oarlocks,
spilling in hissing streams along the side.
Some flail against it filling their hats,
returning the cold water to the sea,
and others wait with folded hands, their eyes
shut out the moon and practice
the last dream that floods in silence,
which the sea covers and forgets.

THE CATERPILLARS

In the Treetops of the hills near Samsun
the first yellow days of spring appear
in webbed cocoons like paper lanterns strewn—
pale pockets filled with eggs that swell until
the caterpillars thrust their blind heads forth
and nose to tail begin their slow descent
in clouds of yellow pollen.
No one knows why they choose to march
linked across those distant fields,
long arcs in the summer dust, slaves
to a season without end; it comes again,
their innards stain the earth with bile
when their chain is broken by a boot sole
and the rest inch forward without purpose.

The Farm Ghost

The damn stars cut like glass—
they torment me this September evening,
the men talk, mouths filled with chewed-up talk
but my ribs are over-tightening strings,
my back, a broken harp frame in the garden,
my mind, steel wires yanked by the angry fists.
Aeolian breeze you say? For forty days
in a dry month this bastard wind has scraped our bones.
My eye sockets are nests for quail eggs
and the beasts drag their hind quarters
through these fields, the farm-carcasses strewn
like scattered parts at the junk market
pockmark the silent landscape, unperturbed,
exiled—the lime-thick shells of our homes.

The Admiral Recalls

We'd send a dinghy and they'd pull it on its side,
a froth of arms and legs cauldroned in the bay.
The women went down easy, their clothes
filled out and dragged them deep like sinkers,
past the anchor ropes and the buoys.
They crossed their arms and breathed into the seabed;
their babies drifted down like petals, no,
like a handful of breadcrumbs thrown into the sea.
There were hundreds, I could hear them splashing,
the men would try to climb aboard the boats,
they wanted life, but the women were wiser,
watching the wall of flames on the seaboard,
the soldiers with their bayonets and manic eyes,
they sank, their skirts spread out like throw nets.

CAPTAIN MARKOS STAYS BEHIND

The gulls will pick your bones, don't let their plumage
fool you, a sheaf of papers spun by the wind,
their bellies swollen with fish fat and wasted bait.
This rusting hull, these green oarlocks
and salt-pitted rivets are all I know.
See the lines in my hand? No love, no lifeline
hocus pocus and the fortune teller's lie—
just the gut string that cuts the flesh.
I've pulled my life from these deep waters.
If I can't steer there, I won't go.
There are no tombstones in the sea,
this blue silence is the mind of God,
my breath just wind in my own sails,
this floating casket has no cover to be nailed.

STAVROS, PATER FAMILIUS

Who makes the rules for bloodlines, draws
that thin but unshakeable veil of obligation
and its subtle shadow across familial eyes?
He was the eldest, with fewest words
and even fewer exclamations, anger
at deception was the manic urge towards love,
towards shepherding the scattered lives,
the family cast out, slung like lead shot,
pain's traveling sideshow, an ark
dragged across these eastern sands,
launched toward safer islands,
Russias of the mind, Paris, a Greece
that was only home in photographs
and the bombast of stuffed generals.

Melanthe Peeling Onions

Athens, 1935

The cut finger bleeds into a bowl
beside the onion peels, porcelain,
edges chipped bright as blindness
in lime-washed, sun-tormented streets.
She drops the knife, the blood rolls
into the fissures of the glass,
stains them red, the bowl stares back
like a pale, sleepless eyeball,
alcohol-rimmed, pain-stricken, plagued
by reoccurring dreams. The music stops
but the dirge that played on hollowed bones
keeps humming, and the landscape in the window
is draped with the photographer's hood,
black velour, sodium flash, the punishing mind.

ARISTOTELES ON LOVE

The fools who fall in wartime love,
those Romeos and Juliets—
I'd rather drink my piss than play that game
where no one ever wins
and it's stones tossed to the waves
that won't return, and nothing gives.
Poor deluded saps who think
their wives will turn, or wives
who think a Turk will wake up Greek.
I've heard this tune a hundred times
but no one cares what old men think
and no one thinks an old man knows
a thing or two of love and war—
I've tasted blood for both.

STAVROS IN PARIS

Stavros carries the story in his veins
from Pontus to Parisian steeple crosses
jutting like skeletons and cranes
in the weak sky—he counts his losses,
his head is filled with chalk lines that remind
of landscapes persistent as rumors,
sketches of a lifetime left behind.
Sometimes he stops in the rue Réaumur
when the light grouts the cobblestones at dusk
and for a moment he forgets his goal,
imagines his brothers on a ship's ashen deck
as the coast was set alight and burned whole,
Euxinos Pontus, that undecided sea,
floods him on the banks of the Seine.

ARIS

When the children were buried by the apple trees
and my wife's last word cauterized and gone,
I took to the hills, moving like a lizard,
hiding under rocks, eyes—holes in torn canvas.
I swore death on everyone and everything,
death was iron twisted in my side,
a low-flying bird with heavy wings
that rowed itself slowly through the wind
like a trireme launched in the dark.
Thin skin between housework and murder—
our children played together in the streets,
the same shared wine went down our throats
and the same color spilled itself again—
the mirologues, death tunes, waver in the valley.

THE PASHA'S LAST DAYS

The Pasha sleeps on velvet sheets and snores.
His scars, once pink and raised, are flat,
the bent carafes lie scattered on the floor,
his black hair faded, his muscles cloaked with fat.
He rolls and crawls on hands and knees
toward the divan and the water pipe.
Apple, mint, jasmine, those wet dark leaves
smolder in the hookah's coals, the smoke
pale blue, boils in the glass, he breathes
it in and blows out rings that break
against the rafters, those pinched circles
like the mouths of the dead in the street below
whose tongues are packed with rain and clay...
to hell with them...he's leaving in a day.

THE GARDEN

Sinope

There was a stone wall around the garden
and the bougainvillea had erupted over it,
clawing its way into the neighbors' railings
where summer was a riot of fuchsia and thorn,
the bucket pulled cold from the well, its tin
sides bent, a tangle of knots on the handle
promised to keep it coming back.
There were birds in the courtyard, lemon trees
and a pomegranate that dropped its red flowers
to the flagstones, and those that didn't fall
exploded into tiny stars that swelled and cracked
in August, wounded skulls in the branches,
but we didn't see that, or dream that,
or hear the church bells in the trees.

EPILOGUE

Chapel Hill, North Carolina

I'm a name in a progressive scene they dreamt of,
where church steeples and universities wildly spire
from quadrangles of grass and architectured stone.
I never packed with sounds of boot soles at the door,
with the scent of powder and death in my nostrils,
the future a non-existent mass on the horizon.
I'm a name they never spoke, I stepped from the ashes
blind, deaf and dumb to what they saw, still a witness
by some force that drags me toward these hills with nothing
but the shards of words passed on, the crumbling photographs,
the tears that slid from my father and grandfather
through the huge black eyes of paintings and into mine;
that weep when the light breaks on these imaginary cliffs.

ACKNOWLEDGEMENTS

Special thanks to the Civitella Ranieri Foundation for a fellow-ship/residency in Umbertide, Italy where a number of the poems in this book were written.

Substantial selections from this book were published in *Poesia* (Milan), *Epiphany*, *Odyssey* and in an Italian bilingual chapbook published by Casa Grande Editions, Bellinzona, translated by Matteo Campagnoli.

ABOUT THE AUTHOR

Stephanos Papadopoulos was born in 1976 in North Carolina and raised in Athens and Paris. He is the author of *Hôtel-Dieu*, (Sheep Meadow Press) and *Lost Days*, (Leviathan Press, UK / Rattapallax Press, NY). He is editor and co-translator (with Katerina Anghelaki-Rooke) of *Derek Walcott's Selected Poems* published by Kastianiotis Press, 2007. He was awarded a Civitella Ranieri Fellowship in 2010 for *The Black Sea.*